DEDICATED TO MY FAMILY

TART

DEBBY DONNELLY-ADDISON

"The Boho Baker"

Recipe development, photography, illustrations, typesetting, editing, tea making, and everything in between: Debby Donnelly-Addison 2022.

Contents

Introduction

HELLO!

Well, hey there, friend! Thank you for buying this book, in only a few pages time you're going to be knee deep in buttery, tarty goodness. Before we dive head first into this new adventure together, I thought I'd explain why I wrote this, and how I'm going to help you achieve the best results possible. Some designs or techniques may look a bit finickity, but don't worry, I've got your back. This is not about achieving perfection, it's about creating something you can be proud of, and is pretty damn delicious to boot.

Introduction

I've been baking and sugar crafting since opening my shop, Vanilla Nova Cake Boutique, in 2010. Sure, nowadays I have all manner of fancy tools available, we've needed them to help churn out the thousands of wedding and celebration cakes we've produced over the last 12 years. But for the first few years, that was not the case. Almost everything I used came from my home kitchen. Forks for crimping, pizza cutters for trimming icing, cocktail sticks for ruffling petals, in fact, I still use a lot of these today. So that's the mindset I've kept whilst writing this book: with the exception of a couple of cheap moulds, I've not used any specialist equipment or tools. There's the odd ingredient that you may need to buy in, but everything else is pretty basic. I've even used the same tin for every recipe, that way you don't have to faff about adjusting quantities or splash out on assorted bakeware. All you need is one 20cm (8" in old money) round tart/flan tin with a removeable base. That's it. One tin, and we're good to go.

Now, some of you may have skipped ahead to the pretty tart designs in the latter part of this book and be asking "but, Deb, why can't I just buy a supermarket tart and decorate that?" Well guess what, friend, you absolutely can. There is flip all wrong with only doing the parts you enjoy. Just want a yummy dessert but not into decorating? Fine! Want to make your tart using a store bought pastry case? No heckin' problem. This is meant to be enjoyable, so just stick to the parts that bring you joy. Thanks to baking shows and social media, we seem to have quietly accepted that baking is a complex science that must be executed with utmost perfection, but that really is not the case. Yes, there is some methodology that must be followed, but there should not be any shame in things not going to plan. I bake for a living, but let me tell you, I've had bread collapse, icing split, and have even thrown a wedding cake at a wall in frustration. Some days just aren't your day, and that's fine, we've all been there. So when you bought this book, you also bought my silence. Feel free to decorate that wholesale cheesecake, or just make a bowl of tart filling and eat it under a blanket whilst binge watching crime documentaries. I won't tell a soul.

I have crammed these pages with hints and tips, from how to get the best out of each recipe, to what to do if things go a bit iffy. This is by no means something to worry about as these recipes rarely go wrong. However, sometimes life gets in the way: a knock at the door could result in a burnt custard, a heatwave could leave you with dry, unusable sugarpaste. As such, I have scattered guidance notes throughout these pages to get you out of any jams and help you get the very best out of your bakes.

Thank you again for buying this book, and don't forget to tag me in any Insta pics of your tart based magnificence at @thebohobaker. I cannot wait to see what you all create.

Deb

Crusts

Getting started

I get it, it can be tempting to play safe and just stick to the refrigerated crusts, but trust me, their baked counterparts aren't as difficult as they may appear. Baked tart cases are generally more stable, provide a thinner, crispier crust, and take less time to set. Plus, I'm going to teach you how to make them in the easiest way possible. Huzzah.

In this chapter, you will find six baked tart crusts and six refrigerated. You can mix and match the fillings as you wish, although like the Cilla Black of tarts that I am, I've added recommended pairings over in the fillings section.

COLD CRUSTS

Refrigerated crusts are an excellent option for baking with kids, or if you're just not fussed on working with heat. As long as you're mindful of crumb size (we'll get to that in a second) and ensure the crust has ample time to chill, you really can't go wrong. With the exception of the Marshmallow Cereal crust (which is far more pliable that the others), it's important that you break down the dry ingredient as much as possible. A quick blitz in a food processor is ideal, but if you don't have one to hand, tip the cereal/biscuits into a food-safe bag, cover with a tea towel, and give it a ruddy good bash with a rolling pin.

You don't need to grease the tin before using, the crust will be firm enough to slide right out. If it feels a little stuck after chilling, just flip the tin over and run a knife through the seam beneath the base before placing the tin on top of a mug and sliding the tin away from the crust.

Getting started

BAKED CRUSTS

There's the traditional way of lining a tart tin, or there's the cheat method. Fortunately for you, I'm going to show you both.

THE TRADITIONAL METHOD

- You want to handle your pastry as little as possible, so make sure you have everything out and ready in advance.
- Dust the worktop with as little flour as possible as to ensure you're not adding to the pastry. Roll the dough out to approximately 5mm thick.
- You can transfer the dough to the tin by sliding a large pastry scraper underneath or placing your rolling pin on the edge of the pastry sheet, rolling the dough around the pin, and then unrolling it over the tart case.
- Leave a little pastry overhang when trimming away the excess, this will help accommodate any shrinkage that may occur while the tart is in the oven.
- Finish by baking as per instructions of the recipe.

Getting started

THE SHORTCUT

If you're not into all that floury, roly-poly action then fear not, I have an alternative. Once the tart has been filled, the only visible difference can be seen underneath the base. If your guests are the kind of people who flip their dessert over to check the integrity of the pastry, it's time to find better friends.

There are two ways you can go about lining your tin using this method:

- Roll the pastry into a cylinder and wrap tightly in cling film before refrigerating. When you're ready to line the tart tin, unwrap the pastry and cut the cylinder into 5mm discs. Press the discs into the tart tin, ensuring all edges are sealed.

- The second method is particularly helpful if you have warm hands and struggle to keep pastry cool when handling. Dust the worktop with a little flour and roll the pastry into a sheet approximately 5mm thick. Using a cookie/scone cutter, cut the pastry into discs and use them to line your tart tin. Easy-peasy.

Almond

 60 MINS   BAKED

INGREDIENTS

250G GROUND ALMONDS

60G UNSALTED BUTTER

3TBSP MAPLE SYRUP

½ TSP SALT

METHOD

1. Preheat the oven to 180°/160°(fan) /gas mark 4.

2. Combine the ground almonds and salt in a large bowl.

3. Melt the butter in short spurts in the microwave. Alternatively, you can melt it in a pan over a low heat on the hob but keep an eye on it to ensure it doesn't burn.

4. Pour the melted butter into the bowl of dry ingredients. Add the maple syrup and give the dough a jolly good stir. Turn the dough out onto a sheet of cling film, wrap firmly and refrigerate for 30 minutes.

5. Turn the dough out onto a lightly floured worktop and roll to a thickness of about 5mm. Slide a large pastry lifter under the sheet of dough and transfer it to your tart tin. If you don't have a pastry lifter, slide a knife under the pastry sheet before you attempt to lift it, just to make sure it's not stuck to the worktop. If your pastry tears during the move, don't panic: just patch it up, using the warmth of your hands to seal the edges together. It will taste delicious, nonetheless.

6. Trim the edges of the pastry to approximately 5mm over the top of the tart tin and pop it in the fridge for 10 minutes.

7. Remove the tart case from the fridge and prick the base several times with a fork. Bake in the oven for 12 minutes.

8. Upon removing the tart case from the oven, swiftly transfer the tin to a wire rack and trim the pastry edges. Leave to cool in its tin before removing.

Marshmallow Cereal

2.5 HOURS   **CHILLED**

INGREDIENTS

70G PUFFED RICE CEREAL

100G MARSHMALLOWS

2TBSP MILK

50G SMARTIES, CRUSHED

Tip: Try switching out the Smarties for freeze dried strawberries or chopped dark chocolate.

METHOD

1. Combine the marshmallows and milk in a pan. Gently heat until the marshmallows are transformed into a gloriously silky, sticky mess.
2. Remove the pan from the heat and stir in the puffed rice cereal. Leave the mixture for two minutes before stirring in the Smarties.
3. Fill a deep bowl or pan with a little cold water. Spoon half of the marshmallow mixture into the tart tin. Dip your hands in the water and press the cereal into the grooves of the tin. Add the remaining mixture and work it into the tin, dipping your hands in the cold water as you go (this will prevent sticking). Refrigerate for at least 2 hours, preferably overnight, before filling.

Coconut Macaroon

40 MINS   BAKED

Store bought macaroons can be very sticky, but don't let them fool you into omitting the butter. It will all come together in the oven, trust me.

INGREDIENTS

380G STORE BOUGHT COCONUT MACAROONS

50G UNSALTED BUTTER

METHOD

1. Preheat the oven to 180°/160°(fan)/gas mark 4.
2. Break up the macaroons into as fine a crumb as possible (this may be a little tricky as macaroons can be notoriously moist). Heat the butter in short bursts in the microwave and stir it into the macaroon mixture.
3. Press the macaroon butter mixture into the tart tin. Bake in the oven for 25 minutes.
4. Leave the tart case to cool in its tin for at least 30 minutes before removing. Store in an airtight container until you're ready to add the filling.

Basic Pastry

65 MINS   BAKED

The key to good pastry is keeping it cool and handling it as little as possible. If you have particularly warm hands or are fortunate enough to live in warmer climes, try popping the bowl of flour and cubed butter in the freezer for 15 minutes before you get down to business.

As always, I won't judge you if you opt for pre-packaged shortcrust pastry or even go so far as to buying a pre-baked tart crust from the supermarket. Hell, I don't even care if you buy a frozen cheesecake and decorate that. If any part of the process stresses you out or fails to bring you joy, cheat. Buy the bits you don't like working on and enjoy the bits that you do. I won't tell your mum, promise.

INGREDIENTS

200G PLAIN FLOUR

100G UNSALTED BUTTER, CHILLED AND CUBED

1/2TSP SALT

1-2TBSP ICED WATER

FOR THE CHOCOLATE OPTION:

15G COCOA

METHOD

- In a large bowl, toss the cubed butter in the flour and salt. If it's chocolate pastry you're after, now is the time to add the cocoa.
- Rub the flour into the butter with your fingertips until the mixture resembles rough breadcrumbs. Add a spoonful of iced water and give the mixture a good stir with a butter knife. If the mixture seems a little dry, add another spoonful of water to ease it along.
- Bring the pastry together with your hands, forming it into a chunky disc. Wrap in clingfilm and refrigerate for 30 minutes.
- Preheat the oven to 180°/160° (fan)/gas mark 4. Take the pastry out of the fridge and roll it out to a thickness of approximately 5mm. You may need a little flour to prevent the pastry sticking to the worktop but do try to keep it to a minimum.

- Transfer the pastry to the tart tin, carefully pressing it into the ridges. If it tears a little along the way, don't worry, just use a piece of the offcuts to patch it up.
- Trim the excess pastry so it sits no higher than 5mm over the edges of the tin. Prick the base of the pastry case with a fork and refrigerate for 15 minutes.
- Place a sheet of baking paper in the base of the tart tin and fill with baking beans. Bake for 10 minutes before removing the beans and paper, and baking for a further 5 minutes. Transfer the tin to a wire rack and quickly trim any excess pastry. Leave to cool fully before removing from the tin.

INGREDIENTS

200G PLAIN FLOUR

83G UNSALTED BUTTER

66G SOFT DARK BROWN SUGAR

1TBSP GOLDEN SYRUP

¼ TSP BICARBONATE OF SODA

2TSP GROUND GINGER

60 MIN   BAKED

Gingerbread

METHOD

1. Preheat the oven to 200°/180°(fan)/gas mark 7.
2. Stir together the flour, ground ginger, and bicarbonate of soda. Set the bowl aside.
3. In a small pan over a medium heat, gently melt the sugar, golden syrup, and butter. Keep stirring until you're left with a dark, glossy syrup.
4. Remove the pan from the heat and pour the mixture into the flour. Give it a good stir until you have a soft, squidgy dough.
5. Transfer the dough to a sheet of baking/greaseproof paper (try not to miss this step, it will be a rascal to manage otherwise). Roll the dough out to approximately 5mm thick. In one quick motion, take two edges of the dough covered paper and flip it over into the tart tin. Do not worry if the dough breaks: Gingerbread is fabulously pliable, and you can always patch it up as you go. Remove the paper and press the dough into the tin. Prick the base with a fork and refrigerate for 15 minutes.
6. Bake the gingerbread case in the oven for 15-20 minutes, or until both the edges and base are crisp and golden. Transfer to a wire rack and swiftly trim off any excess gingerbread. Gobble up any offcuts whilst warm, leaving the tart to cool completely before filling.

Pistachio

70 MINS   BAKED

INGREDIENTS

340G PISTACHIOS (SHELLED WEIGHT)

50G CASTER SUGAR

30G UNSALTED BUTTER

¼ TSP SALT

1 EGG

Tip: Try switching out the pistachios for hazelnuts or cashews.

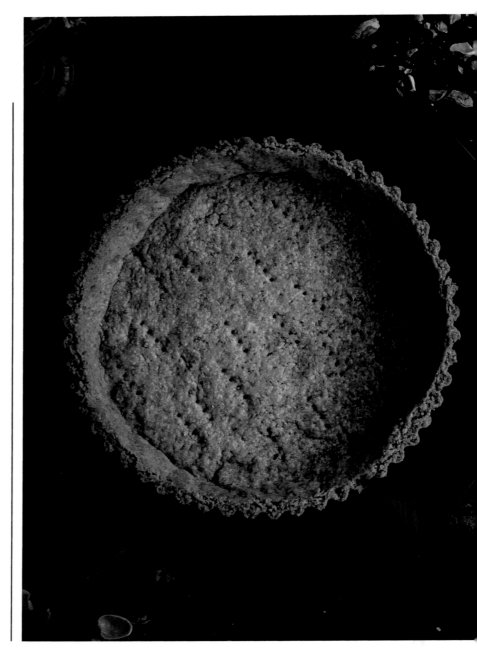

METHOD

1. Blitz the pistachios in a food processor until smooth. Alternatively, place them in a sandwich bag, cover with a tea towel, and channel your rage into bashing them to bits with a rolling pin. Whatever floats your boat.
2. Rub the butter into the ground pistachios. Stir in the salt, caster sugar, and egg to form a sticky dough. Wrap the dough in clingfilm and refrigerate for 30 minutes.
3. Preheat the oven to 180°/160°(fan)/gas mark 4.
4. Roll the dough out onto a lightly floured worktop. Transfer to the tart tin and prick the base several times with a fork. Refrigerate for a further 15 minutes.
5. Bake the tart case in the preheated oven for 20-25 minutes, or until the edges begin to crisp. Leave to cool completely on a wire rack.

Chocolate Caramel Cornflake

2.5 HOURS

CHILLED

INGREDIENTS

120G CORNFLAKES, SLIGHTLY
CRUSHED

160G MARS BARS, CHOPPED

2 TBSP MILK

METHOD

1. Heat a little water in a pan on the hob. Place the chopped Mars bars and milk in a heatproof bowl and place it on top of the pan, making sure the base of the bowl doesn't touch the water. Stir the mixture until it has loosened into a smooth, chocolatey caramel goo.
2. Remove the bowl from the simmering pan and stir in the crushed cornflakes. Spoon the mixture into the tart tin, using the back of a spoon to ease it into the ridges and base. Leave to set in the fridge for at least two hours before using.

Lemon & Lime

75 MINS

BAKED

INGREDIENTS

66G CASTER SUGAR

2TSP LEMON ZEST

1TSP LIME ZEST

190G PLAIN FLOUR

¼ TSP SALT

112G UNSALTED BUTTER,
CHILLED AND CUBED

1 EGG

1-2 TBSP CHILLED WATER

METHOD

1. Toss the cubed butter into the flour, salt, and zest, giving the bowl a good shake.
2. Using the tips of your fingers, rub the butter into the dry ingredients. Stir in the egg to form a soft pastry. If the mixture seems a little dry, add a spoonful or two of water to bring it together.
3. Wrap the dough in clingfilm and refrigerate for 30 minutes. In the meantime, preheat the oven to 190°/170°(fan)/gas mark 5.
4. Turn the dough out onto a worktop and roll it out to approximately 5mm in thickness. Carefully transfer the pastry to the tart tin. Prick the base with a fork and refrigerate for 15 minutes.
5. Cover the base of the tart with a sheet of baking paper and fill with baking beans. Bake for 14 minutes before removing the paper and beans, and baking for a further 7 minutes. Leave the pastry to cool completely before removing it from the tin.

INGREDIENTS

125G SALTED PRETZELS

25G ICING SUGAR

30G PLAIN FLOUR

85G UNSALTED BUTTER, SOFTENED

1 EGG YOLK

30 MINS

BAKED

Salted Pretzel

METHOD

1. Preheat the oven the 180°/160° (fan)/gas mark 4.
2. Using a food processor or a heavy serving of elbow grease, blitz the pretzels to crumbs. Stir in the icing sugar, flour, softened butter, and egg yolk, stirring until well combined.
3. Spoon the pretzel mixture into the tart tin, pressing it into the sides and base with the back of a spoon. Bake the case in the oven for 25 minutes before leaving to cool on a wire rack.

Tip: IF the case slumps a little during the bake, just press it back up the sides of the tin with a spoon before cooling.

Oreo Cookie

OVERNIGHT

CHILLED

INGREDIENTS

250G OREO COOKIES

40G MELTED BUTTER

Tip: You can use pretty much any variety of filled biscuit using this recipe: Custard creams and bourbons work particularly well. Jammy Dodgers can get a bit sticky but are well worth the extra cleaning time.

METHOD

1. Place the Oreo cookies in a sandwich bag and cover with a tea towel. Go over the towel several times with a rolling pin until the biscuits are well crushed. You can also use a food processor for this step but be mindful that this mixture gets claggy pretty quickly.
2. Toss the crushed biscuits into a bowl and stir in the melted butter. Transfer the mixture into the tart tin and press firmly with the back of a spoon. Refrigerate overnight before filling.

Basic Biscuit

2.5 HOURS · CHILLED

INGREDIENTS

250G DIGESTIVE/GINGER/
SHORTBREAD BISCUITS

50G GOLDEN CASTER
SUGAR

60G BUTTER, MELTED

METHOD

1. Bash the biscuits into crumbs. Add the golden caster sugar and melted butter, stirring until soft and sticky.
2. Spoon the biscuit mixture into the tart tin and press into the edges and base. Refrigerate until set, preferably overnight. Carefully remove the base from the tin and fill 'er up.

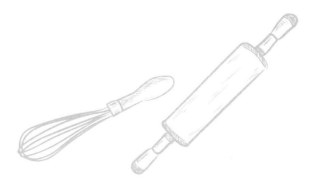

Fillings

Fill 'em up

Now it's time to get cracking on the gooey, silky, creamy loveliness that is the filling. Some are refrigerated, some are baked, all are delicious. Feel free to mix and match as you please.

If this is your first foray into desserts, then I'd recommend you start with the Mascarpone Cream filling: it's so thick that you could technically decorate over it right away (although I'd certainly advise you give it at least a couple of hours in the fridge beforehand). The Marshmallow Cream filling is another great confidence builder, as the gelatine in the marshmallows acts as a setting agent and does all the heavy lifting for you. Both are excellent starting points for the nervous cook.

On first appearances, the baked fillings may seem like a bit of a faff compared to the chilled options, but the beauty of the baked is that you can decorate (and more importantly, eat) them far sooner. If you're a first timer, try the Thyme Baked Custard. It's straightforward and, if you're careful with the heat, never fails.

Finally, ok, I get it, sometimes you're short on time and patience. Hey, that's fine by me, feel free to buy a cheesecake from the supermarket and skip to the next chapter, I promise I won't tell a soul.

Thyme Custard

INGREDIENTS

200ML DOUBLE CREAM

200ML MILK

1 VANILLA POD

3 STEMS OF THYME

6 EGG YOLKS

80G CASTER SUGAR

¼ TSP GRATED NUTMEG

Tip: If your custard splits, place the pan in a shallow basin of cold water and whisk vigorously until it comes back together.

METHOD

1. Preheat the oven to 140°/120° (fan)/gas mark 1.
2. Whisk together the egg yolks and caster sugar until pale and fluffy. Set aside.
3. Combine the cream and milk in a saucepan. Scrape out the vanilla pod and toss the seeds, empty pod, thyme, and nutmeg into the milk. Gently heat for 3-5 minutes, or until the liquid has reduced by a third.
4. Carefully remove the thyme stems and vanilla pod from the mixture. Pour the liquid over the egg and sugar mix, whisking until smooth and glossy. Pour the custard into your prepared tart tin and bake in the oven for 55 minutes. Don't worry if it has a hint of wobble, this will set as it cools.

Recommended crusts: chocolate pastry, gingerbread, or pistachio.

Marshmallow Cream

2 HOURS

CHILLED

INGREDIENTS

100G WHITE MARSHMALLOWS

15ML MILK

260ML DOUBLE CREAM

1TSP VANILLA EXTRACT

Tip: It only takes one pink marshmallow to take this filling from cream to blush. This is fine if you're planning on icing the tart before decorating, but if you're planning on serving this baby au naturel, you might want to bear this in mind when selecting ingredients.

METHOD

1. Pop the marshmallows and milk in a pan and heat until melted. Remove the pan from the heat and leave to cool for a few minutes whilst you prepare the cream.
2. Whip the cream and vanilla extract until soft peaks form. Fold half of the marshmallow mixture into the whipped cream, followed by the second half. Spoon the marshmallow cream into your prepared tart case and refrigerate until set (this should take approximately 2 hours).

Recommended crusts: any at all. This classic filling is a beautiful all rounder, perfect for both sweet and salty crusts.

Mascarpone Cream

2 HOURS   CHILLED

INGREDIENTS

115G MASCARPONE CHEESE

40G CASTER SUGAR

285ML DOUBLE CREAM

1TSP VANILLA EXTRACT

METHOD

1. Whisk together the mascarpone cheese, caster sugar, and vanilla extract.
2. In a separate bowl, whip the double cream until smooth peaks have formed.
3. Gently fold the mascarpone cheese mixture into the whipped cream, being careful not to knock out too much of the air.
4. Transfer the mixture to the tart tin and refrigerate for 2-6 hours before decorating.

Recommended crusts: pretzel, basic biscuit, lemon & lime, coconut macaroon, pistachio, chocolate, or plain pastry.

Chocolate Caramel Ganache

4.5 HOURS

CHILLED

INGREDIENTS

340G DARK CHOCOLATE,
CHOPPED

200ML DOUBLE CREAM

60G UNSALTED BUTTER

200G TINNED CARAMEL

Recommended crusts:
chocolate caramel
cornflake,
chocolate pastry, Oreo
cookie, or pretzel.
.

METHOD

1. Spoon the caramel into the tart case. Refrigerate for 30 minutes.
2. Place the chopped chocolate in a large bowl and set aside. Heat the cream until it's close to boiling point (the edges will start to bubble a little). Pour the hot cream over the chocolate and leave to work its magic for 2 minutes.
3. Add the butter to the chocolate and cream mixture and whisk until smooth. If the chocolate hasn't melted completely, pop the bowl over a pan of barely simmering water and stir continuously until the mixture is free of any pesky lumps.
4. Pour the chocolate ganache into the caramel filled tart. Refrigerate for 4-6 hours before decorating.

INGREDIENTS

120G WHITE CHOCOLATE,
CHOPPED

1TBSP AMARETTO OR
ALMOND EXTRACT

2 MEDIUM EGGS,
SEPARATED

200ML DOUBLE CREAM

45G CASTER SUGAR

4 HOURS   **CHILLED**

Amaretto & White Chocolate

METHOD

1. Melt the white chocolate either in short bursts in the microwave, or in a heatproof dish over a pan of barely simmering water. Stir in the amaretto/almond extract, and egg yolks.
2. Beat the egg whites until white, fluffy, and almost double in volume. Add the sugar a spoonful at a time, beating between additions.
3. Fold half of the egg mix into the melted chocolate before repeating with the other half. Gently transfer the mousse mixture into the tart case and refrigerate for 4-6 hours.

Recommended crusts: basic biscuit, chocolate pastry, pretzel, or plain pastry.

Lemon Zest

70 MIN

BAKED

INGREDIENTS

4 MEDIUM EGGS PLUS

2 EGG YOLKS

150G CASTER SUGAR

JUICE OF 2 LEMONS

ZEST OF 4 LEMONS

200ML DOUBLE CREAM

METHOD

1. Preheat the oven to 140°/120° (fan)/gas mark 2.
2. Whisk together the ingredients until smooth (a hand whisk is fine for this filling, it doesn't require as much gusto as the chilled ones).
3. Carefully pour the mixture into the tart case and bake in the oven for 45-55 minutes, or until the filling is firm on top with the slightest hint of wobble in the centre.
4. Place the tart on a wire rack and leave to cool completely before removing the tin.

Recommended crusts: lemon & lime, basic pastry, and (more controversially) any of the chocolate based tart cases.

Spiced Blackberry Custard

INGREDIENTS

200ML DOUBLE CREAM

200ML WHOLE MILK

6 EGG YOLKS

80G SOFT DARK BROWN
SUGAR

1TSP GROUND CINNAMON

½ TSP GROUND GINGER

¼ TSP GROUND NUTMEG

100G BLACKBERRIES

METHOD

1. Preheat the oven to 140°/120° (fan)/gas mark 1.
2. Combine the double cream, whole milk, and spices in a pan. Bring to a boil before setting the pan aside to cool for 2 minutes.
3. Beat together the egg yolks and sugar. Carefully pour the hot liquid into the egg mixture, whisking until smooth.
4. Scatter the blackberries in the base of your chosen pastry case. Top with the custard and bake in the oven for 40 minutes. Leave to cool completely before decorating.

Recommended crusts: basic pastry, almond or pistachio. Maybe pretzel, if you're feeling a little adventurous.

60 MIN   BAKED

Cookie Cheesecake

2.5 HOURS

CHILLED

INGREDIENTS

180G CREAM CHEESE

50G ICING SUGAR

1TSP VANILLA EXTRACT

190ML DOUBLE CREAM

12 CHOCOLATE CHIP
COOKIES/OREOS, CHOPPED

Tip: You can use the same beaters for both the whipped cream and the cream cheese. You don't need to ruin your fun baking session with an unwanted mid-mix wash up, just switch bowls and crack on.

METHOD

1. Whisk the cream cheese and vanilla extract until smooth.
2. In a separate bowl, whisk the double cream and icing sugar until thick and softly peaked. Gently fold a third of the cream cheese mixture into the cream, repeating a further two times.
3. Stir the chopped cookies into the cheesecake mixture. Scoop the filling into the tart case, smoothing it in with the back of a spoon. Refrigerate for at least 2 hours before decorating.

Recommended crusts: Oreo cookie. marshmallow cereal, basic biscuit, pretzel, or any of the plain pastry cases.

Strawberry Cream

2 HOURS

CHILLED

INGREDIENTS

150G STRAWBERRIES, HULLED

105G ICING SUGAR

360ML DOUBLE CREAM

Tip: This recipe is compatible with plenty of other fruits: raspberries, blackberries, and cherries are all excellent alternatives for strawberries, if they're not your jam (I couldn't resist, sorry).

METHOD

1. Puree the strawberries by blitzing them in a food processor or giving them a bloody good mash with a fork.
2. Whip the cream and icing sugar until smooth, glossy, and thick. Fold in the strawberry puree to create a blush pink cream filling.
3. Dollop the mixture into the tart case and smooth with the back of spoon. Refrigerate for 2-4 hours before decorating.

Recommended crusts: basic biscuit, marshmallow cereal, pretzel, and either of the plain pastry cases.

Peachberry Custard

45 MINS

BAKED

INGREDIENTS

200G CASTER SUGAR

120ML DOUBLE CREAM

30G PLAIN FLOUR

2 MEDIUM EGGS

1 SMALL TIN OF PEACH SLICES

60G RASPBERRIES

METHOD

1. Preheat the oven to 180°/160° (fan)/gas mark 4.
2. Whisk together the caster sugar, double cream, flour, and eggs.
3. Scatter the peach slices and raspberries across the base of the tart crust.
4. Pour the custard filling over the fruit and bake in the oven for 40 minutes. Leave to cool completely before decorating.

Recommended crusts: plain pastry, almond, or pistachio.

40 MINS **CHILLED**

Black Forest

INGREDIENTS

220ML DOUBLE CREAM

100ML WHOLE MILK

260G DARK CHOCOLATE, CHOPPED

15G CASTER SUGAR

¼ TSP SALT

2 MEDIUM EGGS

80G MIXED BERRIES

METHOD

1. Preheat the oven to 160°/140° (fan)/gas mark 3.
2. Whisk together the caster sugar, salt, and eggs. Set aside.
3. Heat the milk and cream until close to boiling point. Remove the pan from the hob and stir in the chopped dark chocolate, stirring until the chocolate has melted completely.
4. Pour the hot chocolate mixture over the eggs and whisk until smooth. Spoon the mixed berries into the tart case and cover with the chocolate custard.
5. Bake for 20-25 minutes or until slightly firm. Leave to cool completely before decorating.

Recommended crusts: chocolate pastry, plain pastry, or almond, for a bit of a twist.

Salted Caramel

60 MIN   BAKED

INGREDIENTS

400ML DOUBLE CREAM

112G CASTER SUGAR

6 MEDIUM EGG YOLKS

28G MUSCOVADO SUGAR

1 TSP SALT

Recommended crusts:
this filling works with
all of the baked tart
cases. Try chocolate
for decadence or
pretzel for sweet,
salty deliciousness.

METHOD

1. Preheat the oven to 100°C/80°C (fan)/gas mark 1.
2. Whisk together the egg yolks and muscovado sugar. Set aside.
3. Gently heat the caster sugar, resisting the temptation to stir. Give the pan a gently shake from side to side if you must, but do not stir the sugar. You'll only regret it later.
4. Whilst the sugar is on the hob, warm the cream in a separate pan. Once the sugar has transformed into an amber hued syrup, add the cream, whisking continuously. Be warned, this mixture will foam and hiss like nobody's business, so add the cream slowly and keep that whisk going.
5. Remove the caramel pan from the heat and stir in the egg mixture a little at a time.
6. Pour the caramel into the tart case and sprinkle with salt. Bake for 45-55 minutes, or until the caramel is fairly set. Leave to cool and firm completely before decorating.

Getting started

Now for the fun part: tarting it up. You will find the difficulty rating for each design in the top right corner, although we do have templates and all manner of sneaky tips to make even the most complex looking tart as easy as pie. No, easier than pie. Don't stress over the details, the joy of sugar craft is letting your imagination run riot. Pink fox? No problem! Gingerbread village looking like it's been stomped on by Godzilla? Fine, tell everyone that's what you set out to do! This is about fun, not perfection.

COATING

Each tart is covered in 105g of sugarpaste (also known as ready to roll icing/fondant), or 200g icing sugar mixed with a little water. Personally, I prefer sugarpaste for the majority of these projects as it's more durable. If you prefer the latter method, make sure the icing is well set before decorating.

MATERIALS

It is easier and cheaper to keep a small stock of food colourings rather than buying coloured sugarpaste (which often goes hard before you get through it). Please, for the love of tart, do not waste your money on liquid colourings from supermarkets: they provide little depth of colour and can spoil icing. A tub of gel colour costs marginally more, will last over a year and wont ruin your icing/worktops/day.

USING THE TEMPLATES

Trace the template onto a sheet of baking/greaseproof paper. Imprint the image onto the sugarpaste using a tracing wheel or sharp knife. Remove the paper before cutting out the shapes. Voilà, you're ready to decorate.

Fox in the flowers

I've graded this foxy fellow as "intermediate", but he certainly sits at the lower end of that scale. If you're not feeling particularly foxy today, leave him out and just scatter some fresh lavender across the top of the tart (as per the image on the inside cover of the back of this book).

A note on edible flowers: make sure your lavender is from a plant away from traffic or where dogwalkers tend to wander. If you cannot be certain if a plant has been chemically treated, find an edible flower site online and buy some there. Better to be safe

INGREDIENTS

105G WHITE SUGARPASTE

FOR THE FOX:

20G ORANGE SUGARPASTE

5G WHITE SUGARPASTE

1G BLACK SUGARPASTE

1TBSP SUGAR PEARLS/SPRINKLES

FRESH LAVENDER

A LITTLE ICING SUGAR, FOR

DUSTING

METHOD

- Sprinkle a thin layer of icing sugar over your work top and roll out the white sugarpaste. Using the tart tin base as a template, run a sharp knife or pizza cutter around the edge to create a 20cm circle.
- Transfer the icing circle to the top of the tart, retaining the offcuts for later.
- Using a sheet of greaseproof/baking paper, trace the fox outline from the templates chapter at the back of this book.
- Roll out the orange sugarpaste. Place the fox template on top and run a tracing wheel or knife around the edges. Remove the template and carefully cut out the fox shape.
- Adhere the fox to the top of the tart using a paint brush dipped in a little water. Use the same stencil to trace and cut out the detail pieces from the remaining white icing.
- Use a little water to glue the white details to our foxy fellow. Roll two little eyes out of black icing and top with a dab of white to make them sparkle. Use the remaining black icing to make his nose.
- Scatter fresh lavender over the top of the tart, leaving space for the fox to peek out. If you don't have lavender to hand, fresh herbs will also look lovely.
- Add a few sugar sprinkles to finish.

Summer Wreath

EASY

This is, hands down, one of my all time favourite designs. It's simple, takes minutes to complete, and always looks lovely. You can use any berries (hell, I've even made it with chocolates instead of fruit), and mix and match as you please. If you've got an occasion coming up and are feeling particularly creative, you could write a message in the centre of the wreath using royal icing or a little edible lustre mixed with rejuvenator spirit/vodka (seriously).

INGREDIENTS

105G WHITE SUGARPASTE

60G RASPBERRIES

50G BLUEBERRIES

60G STRAWBERRIES

FRESH MINT

MINT FLOWERS, IF IN SEASON

ICING SUGAR, FOR DUSTING

METHOD

- Gently wash the fruit in a little water.
- Slice the strawberries in half, leaving the stalks intact if you wish.
- Sprinkle the worktop with a little icing sugar and roll out the white sugarpaste. Place the base of the tart tin on top of the icing and run a sharp knife or pizza cutter around the edge. Place the icing circle on top of the tart.
- Create a wreath by scattering the berries around the perimeter of the tart. Add a few fresh mint leaves and mint flowers (if in season) to finish,

Tip: For a boozy bonus, macerate the berries. The night before you're planning on decorating, place the berries in a bowl and cover with 30g sugar and 60ml champagne, prosecco, or brandy. Give the mixture a quick stir, cover, and refrigerate overnight. Decorate the tart with the macerated berries, saving the remaining syrup to drizzle over each slice upon serving.

Watercolour Petals

EASY

Sometimes the simplest techniques produce the most stunning results. A dib dib here and a dab dab there, and voilà, a beautiful piece of tart art. I prefer to use powder colours for this, but gels work just fine as long as you use them sparingly.

A note on flowers: although the watercolour image resembles hydrangeas, stick to rose petals for the decoration. Hydrangea flowers are not food safe, so it's best to keep them off.

INGREDIENTS

105G WHITE SUGARPASTE

PINK, GREEN, DUSKY ROSE, AND

YELLOW FOOD COLOURING

REJUVENATOR SPIRIT/VODKA

EDIBLE FLOWER PETALS OR SUGAR

PETALS MADE FROM SUGARPASTE

TINTED WITH PINK FOOD

COLOURING

METHOD

- Roll out the white sugarpaste. Place the base of the tart tin over the icing and run a sharp knife or pizza cutter around the edges. Pop the icing circle on top of the tart.
- Mix a little dusky rose colouring with a dash of rejuvenator spirit to loosen. If you're using powder colours, add a little extra liquid to create a water colour effect.
- Take your paintbrush and dab clouds of colour across the lower sections of the tart, almost as though you're painting big, blousy bundles of hydrangeas.
- Mix a little yellow colouring and dab away between the pink areas. Don't worry if you make any mistakes, you can cover any booboos with petals later.
- Use the brighter pink to highlight the dusky rose areas. Dab towards the tops of the bundles, where the sunlight would naturally hit. Use the green to add some leaves.
- Finish with a scattering of edible flower petals before serving.

Pup Tart

Two sausage dogs, wearing shades, floating in a pool. I mean, what more could you want out of a tart?

We're using the templates slightly differently this time, referring to them as a sizing reference rather than a stencil for cutting. I like to make everything on top of the stencil first before transferring the decorations to the tart and adding the sprinkles. You can also make the decorative pieces a few days ahead if you wish, just keep them on sheet of greaseproof paper so they're easily transferrable when it's time to serve up.

INGREDIENTS

105G BLUE SUGARPASTE

30G IVORY SUGARPASTE

10G HOT PINK SUGARPASTE

1G PALE PINK SUGARPASTE

5G PURPLE SUGARPASTE

BLACK EDIBLE LUSTRE DUST

REJUVENATOR SPIRIT

30G MULTICOLOURED SPRINKLES

METHOD

- Roll out the blue sugarpaste. Place the base of the tart tin over the icing and cut around the edge with a sharp knife or pizza wheel. Pop the blue disc on top of the tart.
- Trace over the Pup Tart template at the back of this book. Take the hot pink sugarpaste and mould it into a rectangle, using the template as a guide. Use the blunt side of a knife to create a few seams across the rectangle. Boom, now you have a pool float.
- Take a portion of the ivory sugarpaste and roll it into a cylinder the size and length of your first sausage dog. Stick the sausage to the pool float using a paint brush dipped in water.
- Using a little more ivory sugarpaste, hand mould the head, paws, tail, and ears of your pool float pooch, sticking them together with a dab of water.
- Repeat the previous two steps to create your second sausage dog. Pop him in the "water" alongside his friend. Roll the purple sugarpaste into a tube and place it over the second dog to create his water donut.
- Mix a small amount of black edible lustre dust with rejuvenator spirit and paint our pool pal's noses, paws, sunglasses, and cheeky grins. For a 3D effect, mould the sunglasses out of left over ivory icing before painting black.
- Run a damp paintbrush around the perimeter of the tart and cover with sprinkles. If you have any star/fun shaped sprinkles to hand, you can use some to decorate the pool donut.

Snow Stag

A winter favourite, this serene scene is incredibly easy to put together, I've used flower paste for the stag as it is tougher and sets harder than regular sugarpaste. However, if you happen to buy a 200g bar of chocolate instead of 150g, you can melt some of the left over squares to create the stag instead. I personally prefer to use flower paste as it has a little stretch and is less brittle than chocolate, but just run with whatever you have to hand.

INGREDIENTS

150G WHITE CHOCOLATE

35ML DOUBLE CREAM

5G WHITE FLOWER PASTE

6 SPRIGS FRESH ROSEMARY

1TBSP SUGAR PEARLS/SPRINKLES

1TBSP SNOWFLAKE SPRINKLES

GOLD EDIBLE LUSTRE DUST

EDIBLE SHIMMER DUST

METHOD

- Take the fluffiest brush you own and dust the stag mould with gold edible lustre. Roll the flower paste between your palms to soften slightly. Press the paste into your stag mould, running a sharp knife over the back to remove any excess. Pop the mould in the freezer for at least one hour.
- Roughly chop the white chocolate before transferring it to a large bowl. Heat the cream until it's just about to hit boiling point (small bubbles will be forming around the edges of the pan). Pour the hot cream over the chopped chocolate and leave to stand for two minutes.
- Fold the chocolate and cream together to create a smooth ganache. If the chocolate has failed to fully melt, place the bowl over a pan of barely simmering water, stirring continuously until smooth. Leave to cool.
- Once the ganache has cooled enough to reach a spreadable texture (think margarine fresh out of the fridge), spread a rough layer across the top of the tart. Refrigerate for 20 minutes before adding a second, rougher layer across the bottom section of the tart.
- Place the stag mould face down on a piece of baking paper. Carefully peel the mould away to reveal the golden stag below.
- Transfer the stag to the centre of the tart. Layer up the rosemary sprigs to create two fir trees before giving them a heavy dusting of edible shimmer powder. Add the sprinkles and snowflakes before finishing with a final flourish of shimmer.

Petal & Pistachio

Great news, friends, it's bonus recipe time: Pistachio and rose may be a niche combination, but it would be absolutely criminal of me not to include one of my favourite recommendations in this book. Start with the pistachio crust, no amendments necessary. Next, jump to the chocolate and caramel filling, but leave out the caramel and add a teaspoon of rose extract to the chocolate ganache before pouring it into tart base. Leave to set before decorating as per this recipe. Beautiful.

INGREDIENTS

105G WHITE SUGARPASTE

40G ICING SUGAR

10G UNSALTED BUTTER

1/2 TSP VANILLA EXTRACT

1TSP MILK

5G EDIBLE DRIED FLOWERS

5G PISTACHIOS, CHOPPED

EXTRA ICING SUGAR, FOR DUSTING

METHOD

- Make the buttercream by whisking together the icing sugar, unsalted butter, vanilla extract, and milk. Set aside.
- Sprinkle a little icing sugar over your worktop and roll out the white sugarpaste. Using the tart tin base as a template, cut a 20cm circle out of the icing. Place the icing disc on top of the tart.
- Load up your palette knife (of the back of a spoon, if you don't have one) with buttercream. Press the buttercream onto the icing base and pull the implement away, slowly releasing the pressure as you go. This will create a loose petal/fan effect.
- Repeat the previous step until you've no buttercream left. Sprinkle the rose petals and chopped pistachios over the buttercream petals, and serve.

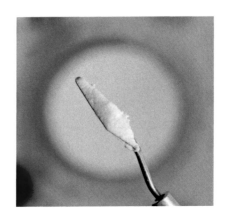
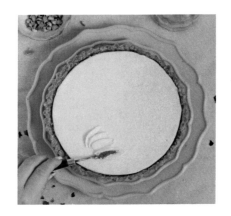
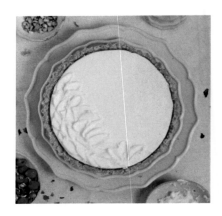

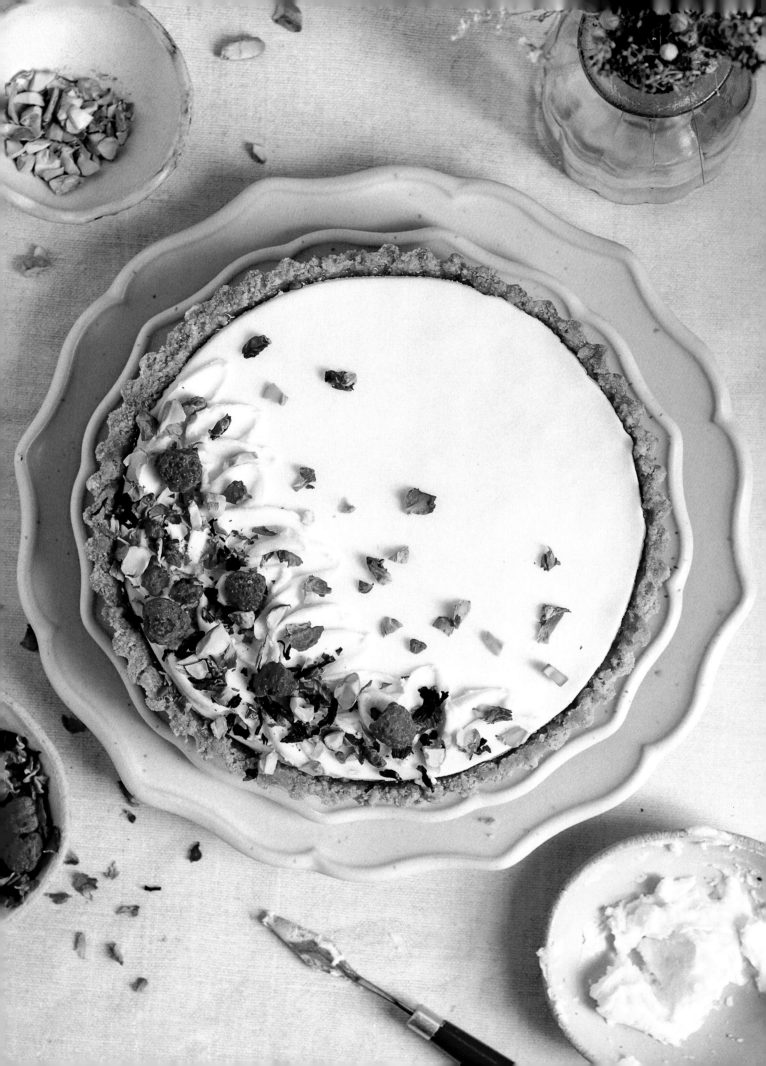

Teddy Time Tart

EASY

If you go down to the woods today, you're sure of a big surprise... A birthday favourite, my Teddy Time Tart is bright, fun, and easy freakin' peasy. The shapes are pretty basic, meaning you may get away with not using the template if you can't be bothered cutting it out: a saucer and egg cup make excellent guides for the face and ears, a mug for his fluffy snout, with the other pieces formed freehand.

INGREDIENTS

105G WHITE SUGARPASTE

50G BROWN SUGARPASTE

5G IVORY SUGARPASTE

50G WHITE SUGARPASTE TINTED

PINK, ORANGE, BLUE, & PURPLE

1TBSP SUGAR PEARLS/SPRINKLES

A LITTLE ICING SUGAR, FOR

DUSTING

METHOD

- Roll out the white sugarpaste on a lightly sugared worksurface. Place the base of your tart tin over the top and run a knife or pizza cutter around the edges. Pop the icing disc on top of your tart.
- Trace the teddy bear template onto a sheet of baking/greaseproof paper. Roll out the brown icing and lay the stencil over the top. Create an imprint of the bear by running a tracing wheel or sharp knife over the outline. Remove the stencil and cut out the teddy.
- Repeat the previous step with the pink, white, and black icings to create the rest of the teddy details.
- Dip a paintbrush in water and use it to stick the ted to the bottom right side of the tart. Cut a selection of flowers out of different coloured icings and use them to frame our teddy friend. Dab the centre of each flower with water and add a sugar pearl to finish.

Tip: If you haven't any brown icing, cocoa powder kneaded into sugarpaste works just as well.

Goodnight, Moon

This tart involves a peculiar (yet simple) technique for edible tissue. Sure, you could make the clouds from sugarpaste, but they would lack the airy, ethereal quality of the tissue. I use this same material on wedding and celebration cakes as it makes a beautiful filler detail between flowers and sugar decorations. A friend of mine did suggest that I just use prawn crackers instead. No. Please, don't do that. Just, no.

INGREDIENTS

105G NAVY SUGARPASTE

40G WHITE SUGARPASTE

1 SHEET WAFER PAPER

GOLD FOOD COLOURING

A LITTLE ICING SUGAR, FOR DUSTING

METHOD

- Sprinkle a thin layer of icing sugar over your work top and roll out the navy sugarpaste. Using the tart tin base as a template, run a sharp knife or pizza cutter around the edge to create a 20cm circle.
- Transfer the icing circle to the top of the tart.
- Trace the moon template onto a sheet of greaseproof/baking paper. Imprint the moon motif into the white icing by placing the stencil on top and running a knife or tracing wheel over the outline.
- Use a damp paintbrush to stick the moon to the tart. Cut out some sugar stars and add them to the tart before painting the details with the gold food colouring,
- Tear up the wafer paper and blitz it in a blender with 100ml water.
- Place a dry frying pan over a medium heat. Add a tablespoon of the paper mixture and cook for 1 minute, or until the water has evaporated and you're left with edible tissue paper. Repeat with the rest of the mixture.
- Tear the edible tissue into pieces and place them on the tart to create your ethereal, edible clouds.

Winter Village

The quickest and easiest way to achieve this design is to make the gingerbread tart base with the chocolate filling, and use the dough offcuts for the village. However, I'm leaving nothing to chance here: for all I know you may have gone completely rogue and be crafting this design on a peachberry custard filling in a pistachio base. I've no idea how wild you people are. As such, in the interest of you rebels out there, I'm starting this recipe from scratch.

INGREDIENTS

150G DARK CHOCOLATE

200ML DOUBLE CREAM

40G UNSALTED BUTTER

33G DARK BROWN SUGAR

1.5 TBSP GOLDEN SYRUP

100G PLAIN FLOUR

1/2 TSP BICARBONATE OF SODA

1TSP GROUND GINGER

80G ICING SUGAR

1TBSP GOLD STAR SPRINKLES

METHOD

- Preheat the oven to 200C/180C (fan)/gas mark 6.
- Melt the butter, dark brown sugar, and golden syrup in a pan over a medium heat. Remove the pan from the hob and stir in the flour, bicarbonate of soda, and ginger. Give the dough a quick knead to bring it together fully.
- Press the dough into the crevices of the winter village mould (see supplier list). Refrigerate for 30 minutes.
- Bake the gingerbread in its mould for 10 minutes. Leave to cool on a wire rack before unmoulding.
- Chop the dark chocolate and transfer it to a large bowl. Heat the double cream until it just about hits boiling point. Pour the hot cream over the chocolate and leave it to settle in for 2 minutes before stirring. If the chocolate has not fully melted, place the bowl over a pan of barely simmering water and stir continuously until you have a smooth, creamy ganache. Leave to cool for one hour.
- Spread the ganache over the top of the tart. Gently place a sheet of baking paper over two thirds of the tart, giving the exposed third a good dusting of icing sugar. Remove the paper and transfer the gingerbread village to the tart.
- Finish by adding a scattering of gold stars and a light sprinkling of sugar snow across the sky and roofrops.

Fluttering Fans

EASY

I love this effect because (a) it looks FANCY, and (b), it's so much easier than it looks. You will need a 2" circular punch (stockists listed at the back of this book), but if you're in a bit of a jam you could always draw around a beaker and cut the circles out with scissors. Alternatively, you could alter the design by cutting the paper into squares. There are no rules here, just go with whatever is easiest for you.

INGREDIENTS

105G WHITE SUGARPASTE

5 A4 SHEETS OF WAFER PAPER

1 TBSP WHITE SPRINKLES

A LITTLE ICING SUGAR, FOR

DUSTING

METHOD

- Dust your worktop with icing sugar and roll out the white sugarpaste. Pop the tart tin base on top of the icing and run a knife or pizza cutter around the edge. Transfer the icing disc to the top of the tart.
- Using your paper punch or scissors, cut as many discs as possible out of the wafer paper sheets.
- Tear up the remnants from one of the wafer paper sheets. Pop it in a bowl with 50ml water and stir to create a thick, gloopy glue.
- Take a paper disc and paint a stripe of glue down the centre. Top with a second disc and repeat 4 more times. Run one last stripe of glue down the centre of the top disc and fold the bundle in half, creating a semi-circular, fluffy fan.
- Repeat with the remaining paper discs until you have several paper fans.
- Attach the fans to the tart by brushing the underside seam with a little water. I like to bundle them up on jaunty angles, but feel free to run with whatever looks good to you.
- Finish by adding a few sugar sprinkles to the blank side of the tart.

Up & Away

Oh to be swept away by a bunch of balloons into a candy floss sky... I've no doubt this little chap will float into a safe landing on a squidgy soft sugar cloud once he's finished his adventures. If you can't get hold of candy floss, you can find jars of marshmallow fluff at most supermarkets (often wedged between jams and jars of chocolate spread). It's not as airy as candy floss, but it's just as ethereal if you spoon it on carefully.

INGREDIENTS

105G WHITE SUGARPASTE

20G CARAMEL SUGARPASTE

5G PINK SUGARPASTE

1G BLACK SUGARPASTE

1G WHITE SUGARPASTE

10G CANDY FLOSS

BLUE FOOD COLOURING

REJUVENATOR SPIRIT

20G GRAPES, HALVED

A LITTLE ICING SUGAR, FOR

DUSTING

METHOD

- Dust your worktop with icing sugar and roll out the white sugarpaste. Using the tart tin base as a guide, cut out a 20cm icing circle and place it on top of your tart.
- Mix a dash of blue food colouring with a teaspoon of rejuvenator spirit/clear alcohol. Using a fluffy paintbrush or clean sponge, dab the top of the tart with blue colouring.
- Trace the mouse template from the back of this book onto greaseproof/baking paper. Roll out the caramel sugarpaste and place the template on top. Use a tracing wheel or small knife to emboss the image before removing the template and cutting around the outline with a sharp knife.
- Roll out the pink sugarpaste. Use the same template to cut out the pieces for our mouse friend's tummy, nose, and other pink details. Stick the pieces to the caramel outline using a drop of water.
- Use the black and remaining white icing to hand mould the eyes, eyebrows, and cheeky grin. Use the pink and white offcuts to roll out a tail and balloon strings.
- Starting from the top and working your way down, stack the sliced grapes (cut side down) to create a balloon formation.
- Finish by tearing the candy floss into clouds and dotting it around the tart. Up and away!

Rosemary Wreath

EASY

An incredibly swift and simple decorating job, I like to make this tart using the gingerbread base and dark chocolate and caramel filling. You can switch out the rosemary for thyme if you wish, or even use a combination of the two. If you catch them in season, fresh cranberries dipped in sugar make an excellent alternative (or addition) to the pomegranate seeds for maximum festiveness.

INGREDIENTS

105G WHITE SUGARPASTE

30G FRESH ROSEMARY

20G POMEGRANATE SEEDS

20G GOLD SPRINKLES

A LITTLE ICING SUGAR, FOR DUSTING

60CM RED RIBBON

METHOD

- Sprinkle a thin layer of icing sugar over your worktop and roll out the white sugarpaste. Using the tart tin base as a guide, run a sharp knife or pizza cutter around the edge to create a 20cm circle. Pop the icing circle on top of the tart.
- Go through your sprigs of rosemary, picking out any pieces that have a natural curve. We want to save these "hero" pieces for the top layer of the wreath.
- Arrange the other pieces of rosemary around the edges of the tart. Place the hero pieces on top to create a smooth, curved finish.
- Scatter the pomegranate seeds and sprinkles over the rosemary like Christmas baubles. Tie the ribbon in a bow and place it at the bottom of the wreath to finish.

Queen Cottontail

This doe-eyed cutie has been crowned with a flurry of fresh flowers (gosh, try saying that in a hurry). If you're feeling particularly creative then you could go ahead and make sugar flowers, but edible blooms are just as beautiful and will finish your tart in a fraction of the time.

INGREDIENTS

105G WHITE SUGARPASTE

65G GREY SUGARPASTE

5G BLACK SUGARPASTE

5G GREEN SUGARPASTE

10G PINK SUGARPASTE

EDIBLE FLOWERS/PETALS

A LITTLE ICING SUGAR, FOR

DUSTING

METHOD

- Dust your worktop with icing sugar and roll out the white sugarpaste. Cut out a 20cm round circle, using the tart tin base as a guide. Place the icing circle on top of your chosen tart.
- Using greaseproof/baking paper, trace the bunny template from the back of this book.
- Roll out the grey sugarpaste and pop the template on top. Trace the pattern into the icing by running a tracing wheel or sharp knife over the outline.
- Stick the grey bunny base to the tart using a little water. Roll out the black, pink, green, and remaining white icing. Use the template to cut out a little bunny nose, eyes, and ears. Add the detail pieces to the grey bunny base, using the template as a guide.
- Run a damp paintbrush over the bunny's forehead. Create a flower crown using edible flowers and petals. Enjoy.

Tip: If you don't have access to edible flowers (or they're simply out of season), you can pull a "Carmen Miranda" and create a crown of fresh fruit instead. Daintier fruit such as redcurrants and blueberries would look beautiful on a bed of strawberry slices and fresh mint leaves.

Playing Dress Up

A rose-scented ballgown, golden confetti, and swags of sugared redcurrant balloons, what more could a gal want?

This is one of those rare occasions where I recommend coating the tart with an icing sugar and water mix rather than sugarpaste icing. It is so much easier to stick the petals to a slightly tacky icing top rather than faff about with edible glue and whatnot. It also helps to separate your petals by size before icing the tart, meaning you can put the skirt together swiftly before the surface sets completely.

INGREDIENTS

200G ICING SUGAR

1 SHEET WAFER PAPER

BLACK FOOD COLOURING

2 STALKS REDCURRANTS

1G BLACK SUGARPASTE

PETALS FROM ONE LARGE RED ROSE

EDIBLE LUSTRE SPRAY

GOLD & WHITE SPRINKLES

1TBSP CASTER SUGAR

METHOD

- Dampen the redcurrants with a little water and sprinkle with caster sugar. Set aside.
- Take a piece of baking/greaseproof paper and trace the template of the lady from the back of this book. Place your sheet of wafer paper over the template and use the black food colouring to paint the design. Leave to dry completely before carefully cutting out.
- Mix the icing sugar with 3tbsp of water, stirring in a spoonful at a time until you have a smooth, spreadable icing (feel free to add more water if necessary).
- Pour the icing over the top of the tart and smooth it out with a palette knife or back of a spoon.
- When the icing has almost set, gently place the wafer paper lady on top of the tart.
- Place one small petal over the top of the dress to create a bodice. Then, starting from the bottom and working your way up, layer the petals into a big, fluffy skirt. Roll a belt out of black sugarpaste and place it over her waistline.
- Scatter gold and white sprinkles like confetti falling over our starlet. Add the sugared redcurrants and spray with edible lustre to finish.

J'adore Paris

Ok, we all knew there was going to be a toughie somewhere within these pages. In all fairness, as long as you stay calm whilst piping, it isn't that difficult. If you're new to royal icing, I'd strongly recommend having a practice first. Using a plate or sheet of greaseproof paper, practice piping straight lines by pressing the nozzle to the surface and applying a gentle pressure to the bag, slowly releasing as you pull the nozzle away. If your nozzle gets clogged, take a pin or skewer and give it a good wiggle to break down whatever is getting in the way. Practice does indeed make perfect, so take your time and be patient. You'll be *magnifique* in two shakes of a croissant,

INGREDIENTS

200G ICING SUGAR	200G STORE BOUGHT ROYAL ICING
BLUE FOOD COLOURING	OR
GOLD FOOD COLOURING	200G ICING SUGAR
PINK EDIBLE PETALS	1 EGG WHITE
	1TSP LEMON JUICE

METHOD

- If you're making your own royal icing, whisk the egg white until thick, white, and fluffy. Fold in 200g icing sugar and the teaspoon of lemon juice, stirring until smooth. Transfer the royal icing to a piping bag fitted with a size no.2 tip. If you don't have a piping tip, you can simply snip a 1mm piece off the end of the piping bag.
- Whisk together the icing sugar and blue food colouring with 3-4 tablespoons of water. Spread the icing over the top of the tart, using the back of a spoon to smooth it over.
- Trace the Eiffel Tower motif onto a sheet of greaseproof paper. Flip the paper over, so the ink is on the opposite side. Take your royal icing bag and carefully pipe over the design. Leave to dry completely.
- There are two ways you can transfer your Eiffel Tower to the tart: The brave may gently slide a palette knife underneath and lift it from the paper. Personally, I like to flip the paper onto the tart itself and carefully peel away the backing.
- Use an extra fine paintbrush to gild the Eiffel Tower with gold food colouring. Use some of the left over royal icing to pipe some clouds across the sky.
- Pipe a zigzag of royal icing around the lower perimeter of the tart, working its way up the left hand size. Cover with edible flower petals and serve.

Bumble Tumble

A tart so pretty it made the cover, this sugar sweet design is a great one for little hands as it requires no special tools or heat. You can use any edible flowers, just make sure they haven't been chemically treated or grown on roadsides (pollution and exhaust fumes do not a delicious flower make). It can be tempting to pick up a tray of pansies from the garden centre, but please don't do this unless you can be absolutely certain that they haven't been treated with any chemical nasties. Home grown or those bought from edible flower specialists are safest and best.

INGREDIENTS

105G WHITE SUGARPASTE

15G YELLOW SUGARPASTE

10G BLACK SUGARPASTE

15G FRESH THYME

FRESH EDIBLE FLOWERS (PANSIES OF VIOLAS ARE IDEAL)

A LITTLE ICING SUGAR, FOR DUSTING

METHOD

- Sprinkle a thin layer of icing sugar over your worktop and roll out the white sugarpaste. Using the tart tin base as a template, run a sharp knife or pizza cutter around the edge to create a 20cm circle. Carefully transfer the icing disc to the top of the tart.
- Divide the yellow sugarpaste into three 5g portions. Roll each piece into an egg shape,
- Using a paintbrush dipped in water, stick the three bumble bodies to the surface of your tart.
- Roll out the black sugarpaste and cut out 6 stripes approximately 5mm wide by 15mm long. Divide the remaining black sugarpaste into three and roll each piece into a ball. Use a damp paintbrush to stick the stripes and noggins onto the bees.
- Use some of the white sugarpaste offcuts to mould 6 teardrop shaped pieces. Moisten the backs of the bees and carefully add the wings.
- Disperse the thyme sprigs across the lower section of the tart. Add the edible flowers and serve.

Chalkboard

Although it's generally ok to flip between gel and powder colours for these projects, this is the one tart where I'd really recommend sticking with an edible lustre dust for that messy, chalky effect. If you only have gel/liquid colours, you can create a similar effect by dusting a little icing sugar around the edges of the tart before painting.

The beauty of this design is you can paint any message you wish. There are plenty of free font generator websites that will transform your chosen sentiment into the style you're after. Just print it off and trace over it as you would with the templates in this book. Birthdays, congratulations, resignations, confessing a crime to the police, this tart can be used to convey a multitude of messages.

INGREDIENTS

105G BLACK SUGARPASTE

WHITE EDIBLE LUSTRE DUST

REJUVENATOR SPIRIT/VODKA

A LITTLE ICING SUGAR, FOR

DUSTING

METHOD

- Sprinkle a thin layer of icing sugar over your worktop and roll out the black sugarpaste. Using the tart tin base as a template, run a sharp knife or pizza cutter around the edge to create a 20cm circle. Pop the black disc on top of your tart.
- Using a sheet of baking/greaseproof paper, trace over the Chalkboard template in the back of this book.
- Place the template over the tart. Gently emboss the pattern into the icing using a tracing wheel or sharp knife.
- Take a small amount of white edible lustre dust and mix with a drop of rejuvenator spirit or clear alcohol. Use a fine paintbrush to carefully paint over the embossed design.
- When the paint has set, dust a small amount of white edible lustre around the edges of the tart to finish.

Tip: You can paint the black icing disc before placing it on top of the tart if you wish. This can be particularly helpful if you have shaky hands or sore wrists.

Blush Sails

EASY

Do spring roll wrappers belong on a dessert? Actually, they do. Dipped in tinted water and left to dry out overnight, this basic ingredient transforms into something undeniably pretty. You can soak them in any colour you wish, although they do look particularly wintery left un-tinted. Just use plain lukewarm water and give them a good dusting with edible shimmer when dry.

INGREDIENTS

105G WHITE SUGARPASTE

3 VIETNAMESE RICE PAPER CIRCLES

GOLD FOOD COLOURING

PINK FOOD COLOURING

EDIBLE SHIMMER DUST

A LITTLE ICING SUGAR, FOR DUSTING

METHOD

- Carefully cut the rice paper circles into eighths. You will also certainly have a few snap along the way but don't panic, I took breakage into consideration when calculating ingredient quantities.
- Take a sheet of greaseproof/baking paper. Give it a good scrunch as you lay it out on the worktop.
- Stir a couple of drops of pink food colouring into a bowl of lukewarm water. Drop a piece of rice paper into the bowl and leave it to soften for 1 minute.
- Carefully remove the rice paper from the bowl and lay it over the crumpled baking paper. Repeat with the remaining rice paper pieces and leave to dry overnight.
- Dust your worktop with icing sugar and roll out the white sugarpaste. Using the tart tin base as a template, cut out a disc of icing and pop it on top of the tart.
- Load a paintbrush with gold food colouring and flick it all over the tart.
- Scatter the pink sails across the left side of the tart, gilding the edges with a little gold food colouring. Spray with edible shimmer dust and serve.

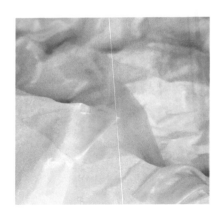

Beehive Bedlam

INTERMEDIATE

How could you not love this little busy bee? Keep him happy with oodles of chocolate honeycomb and creamy fudge pieces (although chocolate chips, crushed nuts, or, dare I say it, crystallised ginger, would work just as well). If you're struggling to get your hands on golden blonde chocolate, white chocolate will do. Just give it an extra brush of gold edible lustre dust when it's done setting

INGREDIENTS

105G WHITE SUGARPASTE

60G GOLDEN BLONDE CHOCOLATE

15G FUDGE CUBES

10G MARZIPAN

2G WHITE SUGARPASTE

2G BLACK SUGARPASTE

GOLD EDIBLE LUSTRE DUST

A LITTLE ICING SUGAR, FOR

DUSTING

METHOD

- Break the golden blonde chocolate into small pieces. You can either melt it in short spurts in the microwave (giving the chocolate a good stir every 20 seconds) or in a heatproof bowl placed over a pan of barely simmering water.
- Pour the melted chocolate over a sheet of clean bubble wrap. Using a palette knife, gently work the chocolate into the crevices between the bubbles. Leave to set completely.
- Dust the worktop with icing sugar and roll out the white sugarpaste. Using the tart tin base as a guide, cut out a 20cm round disc of icing and pop it on top of your tart.
- Peel the bubble wrap away from the chocolate and break it into small shards, Dust the honeycomb with a little gold edible lustre.
- Scatter the honeycomb across the lower part of the tart. Roll the marzipan into a cylinder, tapering off one end. Use the black and white sugarpastes to create the stripes, eyes, legs, and other honeybee details. Give him a little smile using the end of a teaspoon and stick him to the tart using a dab of water.
- Finish by running a damp paintbrush around the edges of the tart and decorating with fudge pieces, Give your honeybee a cube of fudge for his hard work, and serve.

Citrus Meringue

Ok, we're cheating *just* a little here by using store bought meringue nests. If you're the kind of crazy cat who prefers to go au naturel, you can whisk 2 large egg whites to stiff peaks before adding 1tsp cornflour and 110g caster sugar, whisking as you go. Scoop the meringue onto a tray lined with baking paper and pop it in the oven for 30 minutes at 150C/130C (fan)/gas mark 2. Or you could just throw some pre-baked meringues in your supermarket trolley. The power is in your hands,

INGREDIENTS

105G WHITE SUGARPASTE

1 LEMON

1 LIME

1 ORANGE

30G MERINGUE NESTS

A LITTLE ICING SUGAR, FOR

DUSTING

METHOD

- Preheat the oven on its lowest setting. Line a tray with baking paper in preparation.
- Slice the lemon, lime, and orange into 2-5mm thick rounds. Transfer the slices to the baking paper, spreading them out into a single layer. Bake in the oven for one hour, flipping the slices over after 30 minutes. Leave to cool completely on a wire rack.
- Sprinkle a dusting of icing sugar over your worktop and roll out the white sugarpaste. Cut around the tart tin base to create a 20cm disc of icing. Place the disc on top of your tart.
- Arrange the dried citrus slices around the edge of the tart. Crumble the meringue nests into the centre of the tart before giving them a quick blast with a culinary blowtorch.

Tip: The torching of the meringues is for aesthetics only (the meringues are already cooked and fully dried out). As such, you can leave the meringues plain if you don't have a blowtorch to hand.

Rainbow Road

This little guy can slide down his rainbow and into my DM's any time. Feel free to go crazy with colour here, adding sprinkles, stars, glitter, whatever you fancy. He's a unicorn, he was made to be extra.

INGREDIENTS

105G WHITE SUGARPASTE

20G UNSALTED BUTTER

80G ICING SUGAR

10G CANDY FLOSS

GOLD, BLACK, PINK, PURPLE, YELLOW, BLUE, GREEN, AND RED FOOD COLOURING

A LITTLE ICING SUGAR, FOR DUSTING

METHOD

- Sprinkle a thin layer of icing sugar over your worktop and roll out the white sugarpaste. Using the tart tin base as a template, run a sharp knife or pizza cutter around the edge to create a 20cm circle for the top of your tart.
- Whisk together the butter and icing sugar, adding a splash of milk it it feels a little thick. Divide the frosting between 6 bowls (or egg cups, if you have any) and tint with the rainbow colours.
- Heap a spoonful of each colour at the base of the tart. Take a palette knife and spread the frosting in one swift swoosh. Don't worry if it looks a bit wibbly, that's the point. We want it to fade out as it goes.
- Trace the unicorn template onto a sheet of baking/greaseproof paper. Roll out the remaining white sugarpaste and place the template on top. Using a tracing wheel or knife, emboss the outline into the icing. Cut out the unicorn shape and place him on the rainbow. Use the same template to cut out the hooves and unicorn horn. Stick the detail pieces to the unicorn using a damp paintbrush.
- Paint the hooves and horn gold before carefully painting the facial details with the black food colouring.
- Cut out some sugarpaste stars and paint them gold. Tint a little sugarpaste pink and roll it into thin pieces to create the hair. Finally, add some candy floss clouds at the base of the rainbow to finish.

Smooth Sailing

ADVANCED

This may look complicated, but trust me, you can do this! It's more about the cutting out than anything else, just take your time and consider keeping hold of your wrist with your free hand when painting, it does wonders for keeping your brush steady and your mind clear.

INGREDIENTS

105G NAVY SUGARPASTE

50G WHITE SUGARPASTE

10G BROWN SUGARPASTE

20G CARAMEL SUGARPASTE

50G UNSALTED BUTTER

100G ICING SUGAR

BLUE, GOLD, BLACK, AND BROWN FOOD COLOURING

5G ROYAL ICING

A LITTLE ICING SUGAR, FOR DUSTING

METHOD

- Sprinkle a thin layer of icing sugar over your worktop and roll out the navy sugarpaste. Using the tart tin base as a template, run a sharp knife or pizza cutter around the edge to create a 20cm circle for the top of your tart. Splatter with gold food colouring.
- Take a portion of white sugarpaste and press it into the rope mould. Repeat until you have enough rope to frame the tart. Stick the rope pieces down with a dab of water before painting them gold.
- Whisk together the butter, icing sugar, and a dash of blue food colouring. Add a splash of milk if the frosting feels a little thick. Spread the frosting across the bottom half of the tart, saving a little for later.
- Trace the template onto baking/ greaseproof paper. Roll out the brown and caramel sugarpastes and emboss the motif into the icing using a tracing wheel or knife. Carefully cut the pieces out and transfer to the tart. Cover the base of the boat with the left over blue frosting.
- Use the black food colouring to paint the details onto the boat, sails, and banner. Dab some watered down brown food colouring around the edges of the sails and motto for a weathered effect.
- Pipe zigzags of royal icing along the edges of the waves. Dip a paintbrush in water and drag the royal icing away to create sugar seafoam.
- Finally, mould the anchor out of the remaining white sugarpaste. Paint it gold and add it to the bottom left of the tart.

Retro Ink

You can use pre-coloured sugarpaste for this design if you wish, but the colours are used in such small quantities that I find it more cost effective to tint my own. If you do decide to buy coloured sugarpaste, you can make it last a lot longer by keeping it tightly wrapped in tinfoil. Dried or crusted sugarpaste can be revived by trimming away the hard edges and kneading in a little Trex until smooth. Nothing goes to waste on my watch.

INGREDIENTS

140G WHITE SUGARPASTE

PINK, RED, BLUE, BLACK, PURPLE, ORANGE, YELLLOW, AND GREEN FOOD COLOURING

A LITTLE ICING SUGAR, FOR DUSTING

METHOD

- Coat the top of your tart with a 20cm round disc of sugarpaste. Roll out your icing and use the base of the tart tin as a template.
- Divide the remaining icing into 7 evenly sized portions. Use a few drops of each food colour to create pink, red, blue, yellow, purple, orange, and green sugarpastes.
- Trace the Retro Ink template onto a sheet of greaseproof/baking paper.
- Dust your worktop with icing sugar and roll out each of the sugarpaste colours. Use a tracing wheel or sharp knife to emboss each of the tattoo details into their respective sugarpastes. Remove the template and carefully cut the details out of the icing,
- Moisten the top of the tart with a damp paintbrush. Gently transfer the icing pieces, using the template as a placement guide.
- Dip a fine paintbrush into the black food colouring and paint the outlines around each of the tattoos. Don't worry if it's a little wobbly, it's meant to look a bit retro.
- Finish by adding some black speckles to each of the motifs.

Pretty Porcelain

This wedgewood-esque tart is created using nothing but royal icing, water, and a paintbrush. There are two reasons why I haven't created a template for this: Firstly, because I'm not that sort of sociopath to encourage you to pipe royal icing over a sheet of carefully defined lines. You will hate both me and this book in equal measure. Secondly, because the wobblier and wilder the pattern is, the better the overall result. You may not believe it now, but freehand is certainly the more sensible option in this scenario.

INGREDIENTS

105G BLUE SUGARPASTE

1 MEDIUM EGG WHITE

200G ICING SUGAR

1 TBSP WATER

EXTRA ICING SUGAR, FOR DUSTING

METHOD

- Whisk the egg white until fluffed and foamy. Fold in the icing sugar and water before transferring the royal icing to a piping bag.
- Roll out the blue sugarpaste on a light sugared worktop. Cut out a 20cm circle of icing and pop it on top of your tart.
- Snip the end off your piping bag. Pipe out a rough flower, the wobblier, the better. Dip a paintbrush in water and use it to drag the outer edges of the flower towards the centre. Add another four wobbly petals and repeat.
- Continue the pattern across the tart as per the images below. You can fill the negative space with leaves, swirls, and dots, if you prefer a particularly full design. Continue to pipe and spread until you're happy with the final overall tart art.

Rainbow Fish

EASY

This bright, jolly fellow can be dressed up in any assortment of colours (he is a rainbow fish, after all). If you have the extra mixing and washing up time, he would look particularly snazzy in five or six colours with a sprinkling of edible glitter, should you be so bold. If you're not a fan of food colouring, natural tints such as butterfly pea powder, dried beetroot, matcha, and turmeric powder produce an equally delightful result.

INGREDIENTS

60G WHITE SUGARPASTE

200G ICING SUGAR

50G UNSALTED BUTTER

1TSP VANILLA EXTRACT

2 TBSP MILK

2G BLACK SUGARPASTE

THREE FOOD COLOURINGS OF YOUR CHOOSING

METHOD

- Divide the white sugarpaste into four 15g portions. Use two to make the upper and lower fins, one to make the tail, and the final piece to make the lips, eye, and side fin.
- Moisten the tail with a damp paintbrush and stick it on to the tart. Repeat with the upper and lower fins, and mouthpiece.
- Whisk together the icing sugar, butter, vanilla extract, and milk. Divide the buttercream between three bowls and tint each one with a few drops of food colouring.
- Use a palette knife or back of a teaspoon to coat each of the icing details with buttercream.
- Transfer the frostings into three separate piping bags. Snip a 1cm wide opening in the end of each bag. Pipe alternating coloured blobs of buttercream down one side of the fish. Press a teaspoon into each blob and swoosh away to the right (see image below). Pipe another row and repeat until the tart is fully covered.
- Press the eye into the buttercream, adding a small circle of black sugarpaste for the pupil. Add the side fin and cover with frosting to finish.

Buttercream Flowers

EASY

The beauty of this design is that there are no specialist piping techniques involved. Sure, there are plenty of incredible buttercream flower techniques out there, but let's keep it simple. Each flower is created by layering up dots of buttercream, that's it. You could even get away with not using the star nozzle if you don't mind a slightly different look, just layer up those buttercream blobs for a fluffy floral effect.

INGREDIENTS

105G WHITE SUGARPASTE

25G UNSALTED BUTTER

100G ICING SUGAR

PINK, LAVENDER, AND GREEN FOOD

COLOURING

EXTRA ICING SUGAR, FOR DUSTING

EDIBLE SHIMMER SPRAY

1TSP SUGAR PEARLS

METHOD

- Sprinkle a thin layer of icing sugar over your worktop and roll out the white sugarpaste. Using the tart tin base as a template, run a sharp knife or pizza cutter around the edge to create a 20cm circle. Place the icing circle on top of the tart.
- Whisk together the butter and icing sugar to create a stiff buttercream. If it feels a little dry, add a tablespoon of milk to loosen.
- Divide the buttercream between four bowls. It may not look like much, but we only need a small amount of each colour for this design. Tint three of the bowls with with food colouring, leaving the last one plain,
- Transfer the plain buttercream to a piping bag fitted with a small star nozzle. Transfer the coloured frostings to three separate piping bags fitted with no.2 size nozzles or with no nozzles and the end snipped off.
- Pipe several random stalks of green frosting across the lower half of the tart. Add some leaves by piping a dot of buttercream and continuing to squeeze the bag as you pull it away.
- Starting at the top of one of your stalks, pipe a series of lavender dots in a cone shape, tapering off like a head of lavender. Next, take the pink buttercream and pink 5 small dots in a circular formation. Pop a sugar pearl in the centre to create a flower.
- Finally, take the plain buttercream and pipe a cloud of frosting stars at the tops of your two longest stalks. Use any leftover pink and lavender buttercream to add a scattering of polka dots across the canvas. Finish with a spritz of edible lustre spray.

Ombre Wave

EASY

This uncomplicated design is perfect for a peaceful afternoon's baking. I've opted for pinks here, but the ombre waves will look beautiful in any shade. If you have a little more time (and patience) on your hands, this would look particularly lovely in rainbow hues, flowing from red to blue.

INGREDIENTS

105G WHITE SUGARPASTE

FOR THE DECORATION:

90G WHITE SUGARPASTE

FOOD COLOURING OF YOUR CHOICE

1TBSP SUGAR PEARLS/SPRINKLES

A LITTLE ICING SUGAR, FOR

DUSTING

METHOD

- Sprinkle a thin layer of icing sugar over your worktop and roll out 105g of the white sugarpaste. Using the tart tin base as a template, run a sharp knife or pizza cutter around the edge to create a 20cm icing disc. Pop the disc on top of your tart.
- Divide the remaining white sugarpaste into 5 pieces. Use your chosen food colouring to tint 4 of the sugarpaste portions, getting slightly darker as you go.
- Roll out your five shades of sugarpaste. Use a pizza cutter to cut them into a wobbly strips approximately 2cm wide. Don't worry about precision: the wonkier, the better.
- Brush the top of your tart with a little water. Starting with the white pieces, layer the strips from light to dark, trimming the edges as you go.
- Add a few sugar sprinkles to finish.

Wilf the Dog

Just look at that little face! I've created an easy to follow photo guide to make this little chap as simple as possible. For a chocolatey terrier option, add 2tbsp cocoa to the buttercream whilst mixing.

INGREDIENTS

50G UNSALTED BUTTER

200G ICING SUGAR

1TSP VANILLA EXTRACT

2TBSP MILK

10G BLACK SUGARPASTE

2G PINK SUGARPASTE

1G WHITE SUGARPASTE

METHOD

- Whisk together the icing sugar, butter, vanilla extract, and milk, to create a smooth buttercream. Spoon the frosting into a piping bag fitted with a large star nozzle.
- Using the photo guide below, start by piping the ears, followed by the forehead. Pipe his fluffy chin and upper part of his face, followed by his magnificently moustachioed snout.
- Roll two eyes and a nose out of the black sugarpaste. Hand mould the pink sugarpaste into a teardrop shape before pressing the blunt side of a knife down the centre to create a tongue.
- Carefully arrange the eyes, nose, and tongue on our furry friend's face. Dab the eyes with a damp paintbrush and add a dot of white sugarpaste to bring them to life.
- Finish by piping two thick buttercream eyebrows.

Pinkie Pie

I do adore this blushing birdy, but if pink doesn't make you wink, you can switch out the candy melts for regular white chocolate and create an elegant swan. If you find your chocolate is a bit thick or at the early stages of seizing, quickly stir in a drop or two of cooking oil (any type will do) to loosen it up again.

INGREDIENTS

105G WHITE SUGARPASTE

100G PINK CANDY MELTS

5G BLACK SUGARPASTE

GOLD FOOD COLOURING

A LITTLE ICING SUGAR, FOR

DUSTING

METHOD

- Cut out a large sheet of greaseproof paper and trace the flamingo template from the back of this book.
- Tip the candy melts into a heatproof bowl. Melt the chocolate in short bursts in the microwave, stirring every 20 seconds. ideally, you want to melt the chocolate gradually rather than just nuking it. Short bursts and quick stirs are the best way to go about this.
- Drop two tablespoons of chocolate onto the flamingo template, gently spreading until it meets the edges.
- Use a teaspoon to drop dollops of chocolate onto the paper. Using a pastry brush or spoon, spread the chocolate into feathers. Leave to set for 30 minutes,
- Dust the worktop with a little icing sugar and roll out the white sugarpaste. Cut out a 20cm disc of icing and pop it on top of your tart.
- Dunk a paintbrush in gold food colouring and splatter across the tart's surface.
- Carefully peel the chocolate pieces from the paper. Place the flamingo neck piece on top of the icing before layering up the feathers.
- Roll out the black icing and use the template to cut out the beak and eyelashes. Use the white icing offcuts to create the stripe and crown.
- Stick the icing pieces to the tart using a paintbrush dipped in water. Paint the crown with gold food colouring to finish,

Templates

Using the templates

Easy-blooming-peasy. Trace over your chosen template using baking/greaseproof paper. Run a knife or tracing wheel over the outline, remove the paper, and cut out with a sharp knife. Donezo.

TIP

You don't need to trace an individual template for each part of the design. Draw the design in its entirety and re-use it for each piece, the paper can take it as long as you're not too heavy handed.

What's THE **BEST** THAT COULD *Happen?*

Chalkboard

Retro Ink

Fox in the flowers

Smooth Sailing

Pup Tart

Teddy Time Tart

Rainbow Road

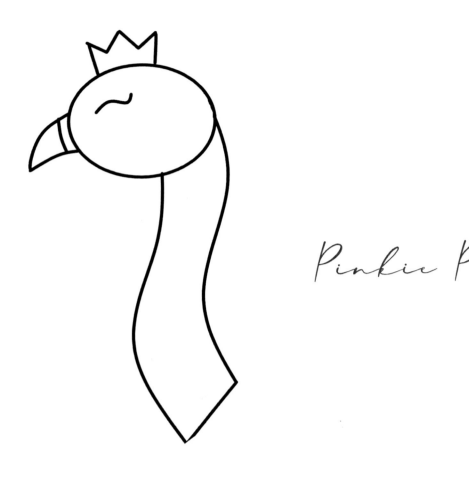

Pinkie Pie

Up & Away

Goodnight, Moon

Queen Cottontail

Playing Dress Up

Paris in Springtime

DONT FORGET TO
SHARE YOUR
CREATIONS WITH
ME ON INSTAGRAM
USING #TARTART
AND
@THEBOHOBAKER

Thank you x

Acknowledgements

This book would never have come into existence had it not been for the encouragement and kindness of so many. For this, I must thank my parents for their insistence that I follow my heart, and not losing their damn minds when I ditched my legal career for cake. Thank you to Dave for easing the load and looking after business whilst I typed, snapped, and edited like my life depended on it. I could not have done this without your support.

Thank you to my brother, Peter, and the many wonderful friends who have provided support and sanity during this journey; Rachel Lightfoot, Harriett Wraite, Chris Williams, Sue Gossage, Siobhan Shea, Suzanne Steele, Sharon Bishop, and Stephen Langstaff, who probably didn't realise what he was starting when he turned to me in court one day and said "you should open a cake shop".

Special thanks to the Pat & Ian Bakewell, for your many kindnesses.

Finally, thank you to Paul Mackenzie, Laura Bartlett, Gemma Langford, and everyone at Booths, Lancashire Life, and House of Coco, for taking a chance on the sweet looking baker who swears like a sailor.

Recommended Suppliers

- Tart tin: I have used the Tala Performance 20cm Fluted Flan Dish for every tart in this book. You will only need one and it will last you forever. You can pick one up at www.talacooking,com, Amazon, or Dunelm.

- Moulds: The mould used for the Winter Village tart is from Karen Davies Sugarcraft. You can order order direct at www.karendaviessugarcraft.co.uk. The stag, anchor, and rope moulds are from www.amazon.com.

- Chocolate: for coloured chocolate decorations, I use PME Candy Buttons. They set relatively quickly yet still allow enough moulding time. For all other chocolate decorations, I use Dr. Oetker or Marks & Spencer cooking chocolate.

- Rice paper sails: Bamboo Tree Vietnamese Rice Paper circles (spring roll wraps), available on Amazon.

- Flutter fans: Edible Wafer Paper by Squires Kitchen. The 2" round paper punch was from www.hobbycraft.co.uk, although similar can be found on Etsy and Amazon.

- Colours: Both the edible lustre dusts and gel food colourings are by Sugarflair and are available online or, if you're in the north west of England, at my shop, Vanilla Nova Cake Boutique. Other brands are available but please do not use supermarket water based colours, the quality just isn't the same.

- Rejuvenator Spirit: I use Sugarflair Rejuvenator, although vodka works just as well.

- Icing: If you're feeling fancy or planning on using the remainder to cover a cake, The Sugarpaste by www.thecakedecoratingcompany.co.uk is terrific. However, as tarts are flat, any generic brand sugarpaste (also known as ready to roll icing) will do.

- Tracing wheel: I use haberdashery tracing wheels as they are sturdy and last a long time (I'm still using my mum's one from the 1970's). You can pick one up online or at a fabric/haberdashery store.